THE 10 MAJOR DYNASTIES OF ANCIENT CHINA

Ancient History 3rd Grade
Children's Ancient History

BABY PROFESSOR
EDUCATION KIDS

CHINA is a broad land, reaching from the deserts of inland Asia and the Himalayan mountains to the Pacific Ocean. Its rulers formed "dynasties" that led China for most of the past 3,000 years. Let's find out about the greatest Chinese dynasties!

A LAND OF DYNASTIES

In Chinese history, a "dynasty" is a series of rulers who all come from the same family. Usually, this means that the later rulers support and extend the plans and projects that were important to the family members who ruled before them.

There were more than twenty dynasties over the last three thousand years of Chinese history, but some did not last very long. Let's look at the ten most important Chinese dynasties.

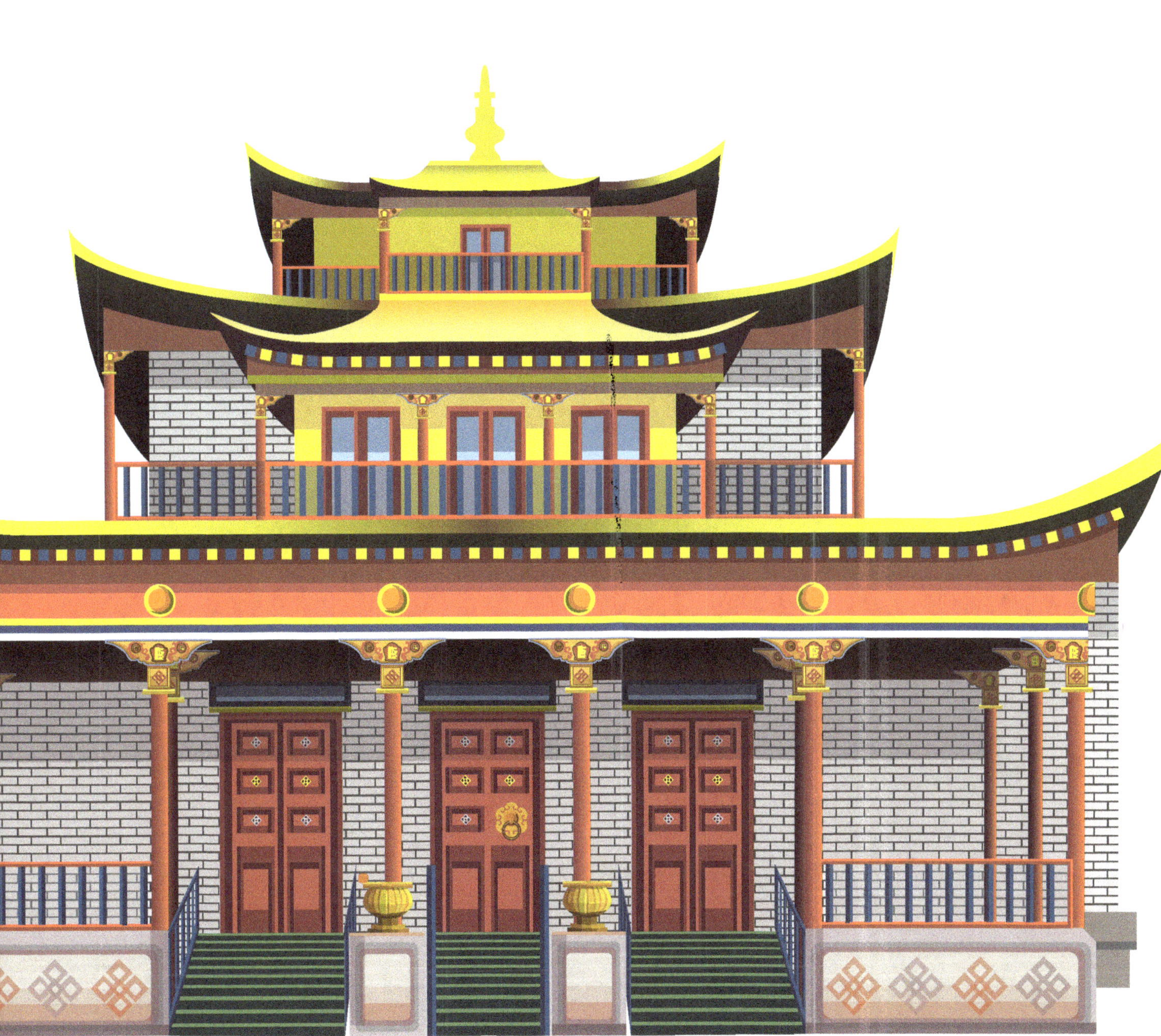

XIA TOMBS

THE EARLY DYNASTIES

1. Xia (2070-1600 BCE)

Although the Chinese people existed before the rise of this dynasty, the Xia Dynasty is considered the first great and consistent government of China. It lasted almost five hundred years, and 17 emperors were members of the dynasty. The Xia Dynasty controlled a large area in north central China, but not all of China.

The first ruler, Yu the Great, decreed that each new emperor should be the best family member available, not the oldest or the richest. However, very soon the dynasty broke this rule, and most of the time when an emperor died his oldest or most powerful son became the new emperor.

YU THE GREAT

XIA DYNASTY POTTERY

During this time people mainly worked as farmers and herders, using tools made of stone and bone. The Chinese started making tools and weapons of bronze during this period.

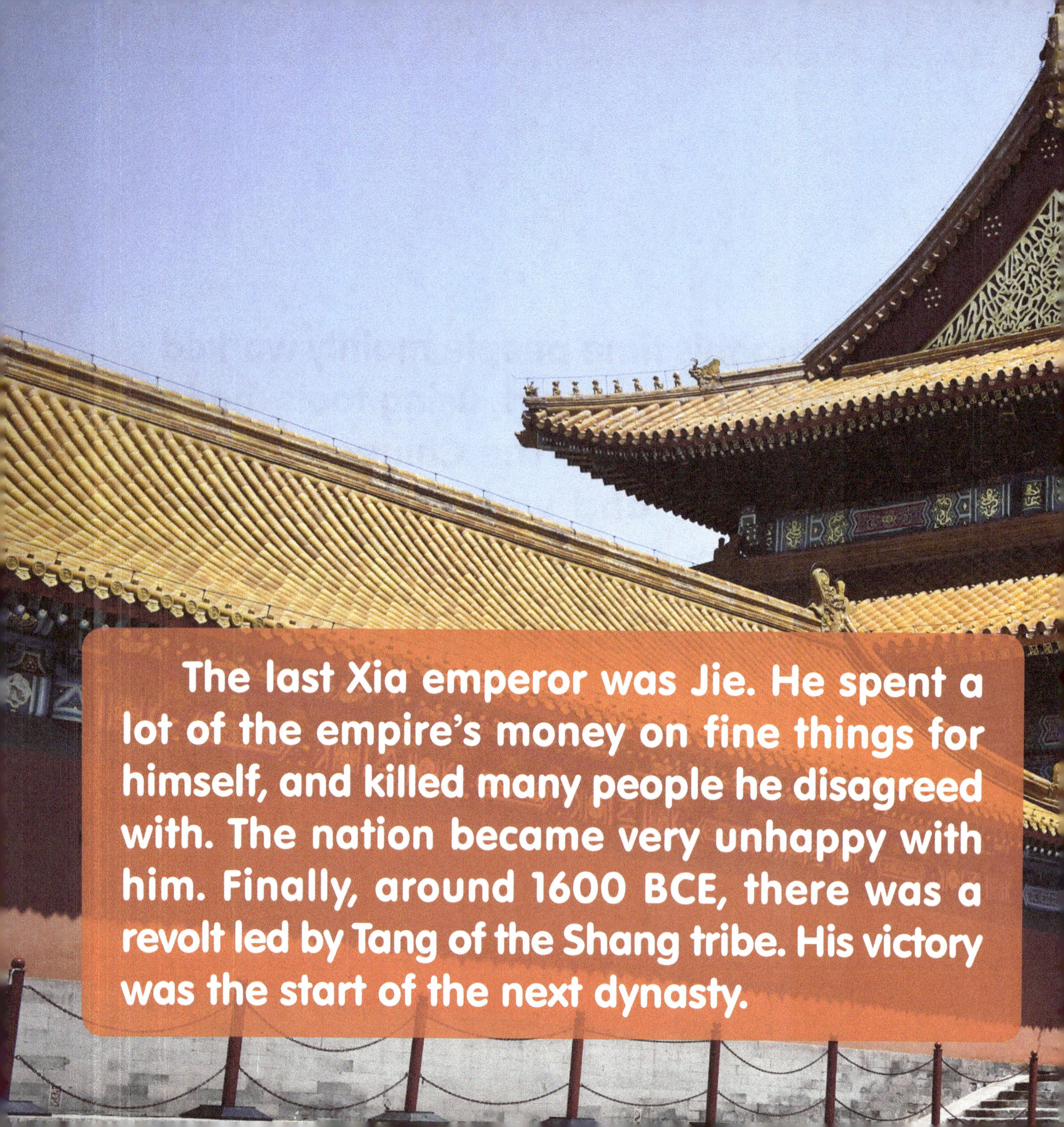

The last Xia emperor was Jie. He spent a lot of the empire's money on fine things for himself, and killed many people he disagreed with. The nation became very unhappy with him. Finally, around 1600 BCE, there was a revolt led by Tang of the Shang tribe. His victory was the start of the next dynasty.

SHANG DYNASTY

DRAGON-SHAPED GONG

2. Shang (1600-1046 BCE)

The Shang Dynasty ruled China for about 600 years, with 30 family members serving as emperor during that time. This dynasty expanded the territory controlled by the central government. People developed pottery, metal-working, and jewelry and decorations made of jewels, bronze, bone, and stone. The earliest written Chinese records come from the time of this dynasty.

Some of the emperors were good and led the country peacefully. Others were cruel or greedy, and things did not go well for the people. The last emperor of the dynasty, Zhou, was so bad that he was overthrown by Wuwang, the founder of the next dynasty.

WUWANG

SHI HUANGDI

3. Zhou (1046-221 BCE)

The Zhou lasted the longest of any Chinese dynasty, for over eight hundred years! There were 37 Zhou dynasty emperors.

For much of this period, China was not under one government. There were the Western and Eastern Zhou territories from 770 to 476 BCE. Then, until the end of the dynasty, China was involved in a series of wars. This time is sometimes called the Warring States period.

Finally, Shi Huangdi unified China under his control, and founded the next dynasty.

4. Qin (221-206 BCE)

The Qin Dynasty did not last very long, but it was very important to the formation of China. The Qin tried to strengthen the way China was governed, to reform the economy and the army, and to correct what the emperor saw as mistakes in Chinese culture. During this time the weights and measures that were used when buying and selling everything from food to clothing became standardized. The name "China" probably comes from the name of this dynasty.

THE GREAT WALL OF CHINA

LIU BANG

Under the Qin, China started to build its most ambitious project, the Great Wall of China, to protect China from raiders from Mongolia and other northern areas. Read more about this amazing structure in the Baby Professor book, Who Built the Great Wall of China?

There was a war between different parts of the dynasty, and finally the part led by Liu Bang won. He established the next great dynasty.

5. Han (206 BCE – 220 CE)

The Han Dynasty was led by 24 emperors over four hundred years. It was a period of great prosperity and growth for China. Victories over other nations and peoples led to expansion far into the west, along the Pacific coast, and north into Korea.

HISTORICAL REMAINS OF HAN DYNASTY GREAT WALL

During this time the Chinese started making paper, invented the rudder for steering ships, and developed the idea of negative numbers (-1, -2, and so on) for use in complicated math problems.

One of the great new things for China under the Han dynasty was the immense trading route called The Silk Road. It was not one road, but many routes joining cities and people all the way from central China to the eastern shore of the Mediterranean Ocean, and even into Europe. Goods, people, and knowledge flowed in both directions along The Silk Road. Learn more in the Baby Professor book **Trade and Commerce in Ancient China – The Grand Canal and the Silk Road.**

SILK ROAD

Toward the end of the dynasty, there was more and more conflict and struggles for power among China's leaders. In the end, the dynasty fell and China experienced a period of great unrest.

THE SIX DYNASTIES

From 220 CE to CE there were six short-lived dynasties that tried to control China. None of them controlled all of what had been China under the Han emperors, and China was not united under a single leader.

Finally, the emperor Wen of the Sui faction rejoined southern and northern China and founded the next great dynasty.

EMPEROR WEN

CHINA UNIFIED AGAIN

6. Sui (581–618)

The Sui Dynasty lasted only 38 years, with only three emperors, and it is mainly important for having reunited China. The government expanded the Great Wall, and created the Grand Canal to help merchants move their goods through the country by ship.

GRAND CANAL

The second emperor, Yang, was a violent and corrupt man, and damaged both the country and his dynasty. Soon after his death, the next great dynasty arose.

帝廣在位十三年
EMPEROR YANG

TANG DYNASTY

7. Tang (618-907)

The time of the Tang Dynasty is sometimes called the Golden Age of China. During this period there were great advances in science, building, trade, the arts, and writing. China still follows many of the cultural practices and political patterns established under the Tang.

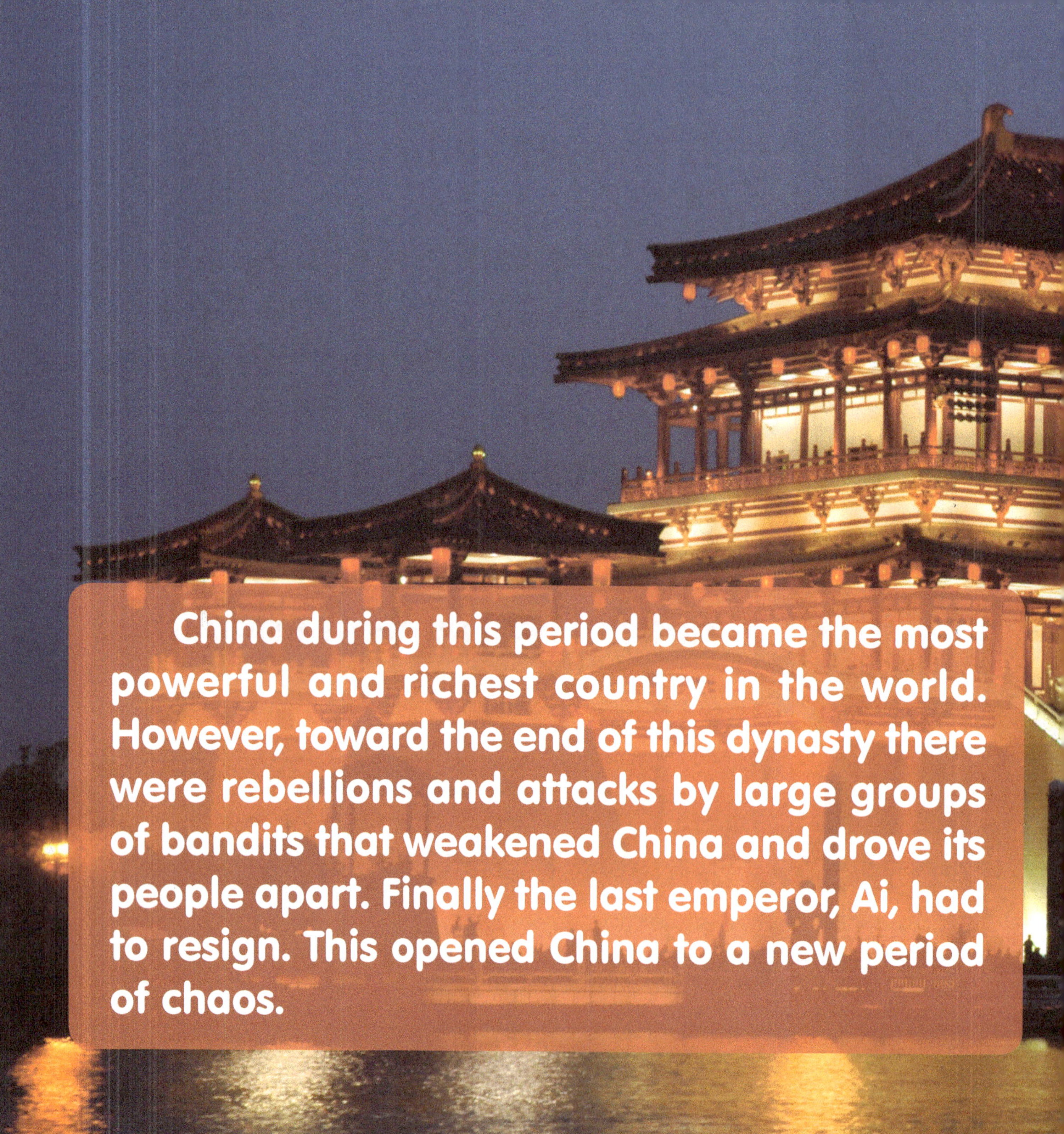

China during this period became the most powerful and richest country in the world. However, toward the end of this dynasty there were rebellions and attacks by large groups of bandits that weakened China and drove its people apart. Finally the last emperor, Ai, had to resign. This opened China to a new period of chaos.

TANG PARADISE CENTER AT NIGHT

THE FIVE DYNASTIES

In 53 years, from 907 to 960, China saw five dynasties and as many as ten kingdoms where there had once been a single empire. All these forces struggled with each other to gain power, and both rich rulers and simple farmers suffered as a result.

Finally one leader gained enough power that he could start the process of reuniting China. He founded the next great dynasty.

THE LATER DYNASTIES

8. Song (960-1279)

General Zhao Kuang-yin was declared emperor by his own army in 960. He was able to reconquer all of China.

Under the Song, China led the world in science, and with inventions like the compass and the printing press.

GENERAL ZHAO KUANG-YIN

The Song Dynasty ended when the Mongols conquered China in 1279. Read about this period, the Yuan Dynasty, in the Baby Professor book Kublai Khan, China's Mongol Emperor.

9. Ming (1368-1644)

Under the Ming Dynasty, China succeeded in ending Mongol control of the country. The Ming extended and strengthened the Great Wall, and ruled an orderly China that was mainly peaceful.

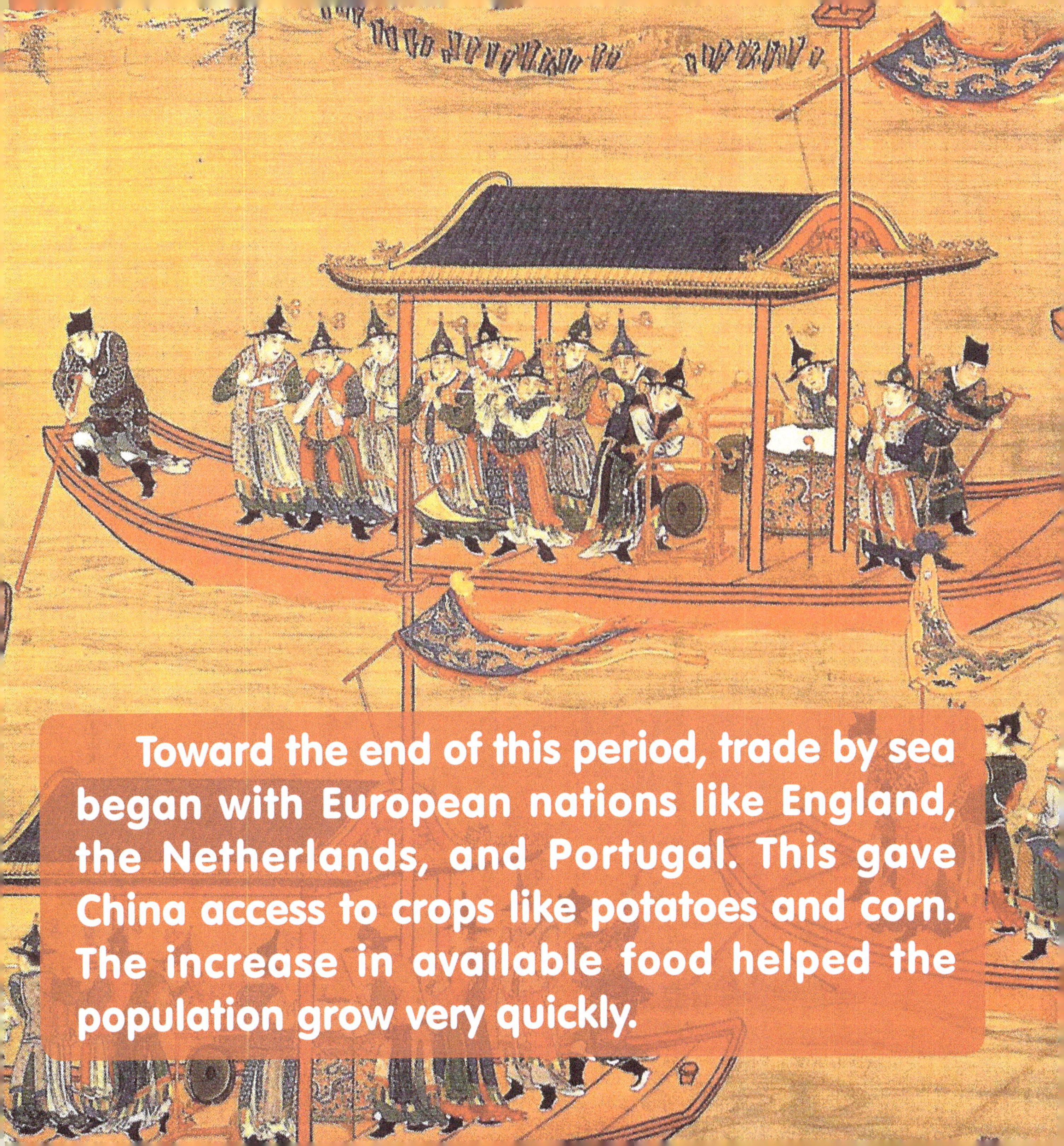

Toward the end of this period, trade by sea began with European nations like England, the Netherlands, and Portugal. This gave China access to crops like potatoes and corn. The increase in available food helped the population grow very quickly.

FORBIDDEN CITY

During this period China built the Forbidden City in the center of the capital, Beijing. This is a huge area of forts, offices, parks, and houses that was the special home of the leaders of China.

Crop failures, famine, and local rebellions led to the end of the dynasty, and opened the way for the last great Chinese dynasty.

10. Qing (1644-1949)

The Qing, or Manchu, Dynasty began when an army of peasants, demanding more food and better working conditions, conquered Beijing. Much of China resisted this new dynasty, which they saw as an invasion by people from Manchuria. It took more than forty years for China to be reunified.

THE IMPERIAL PALACE OF THE QING DYNASTY

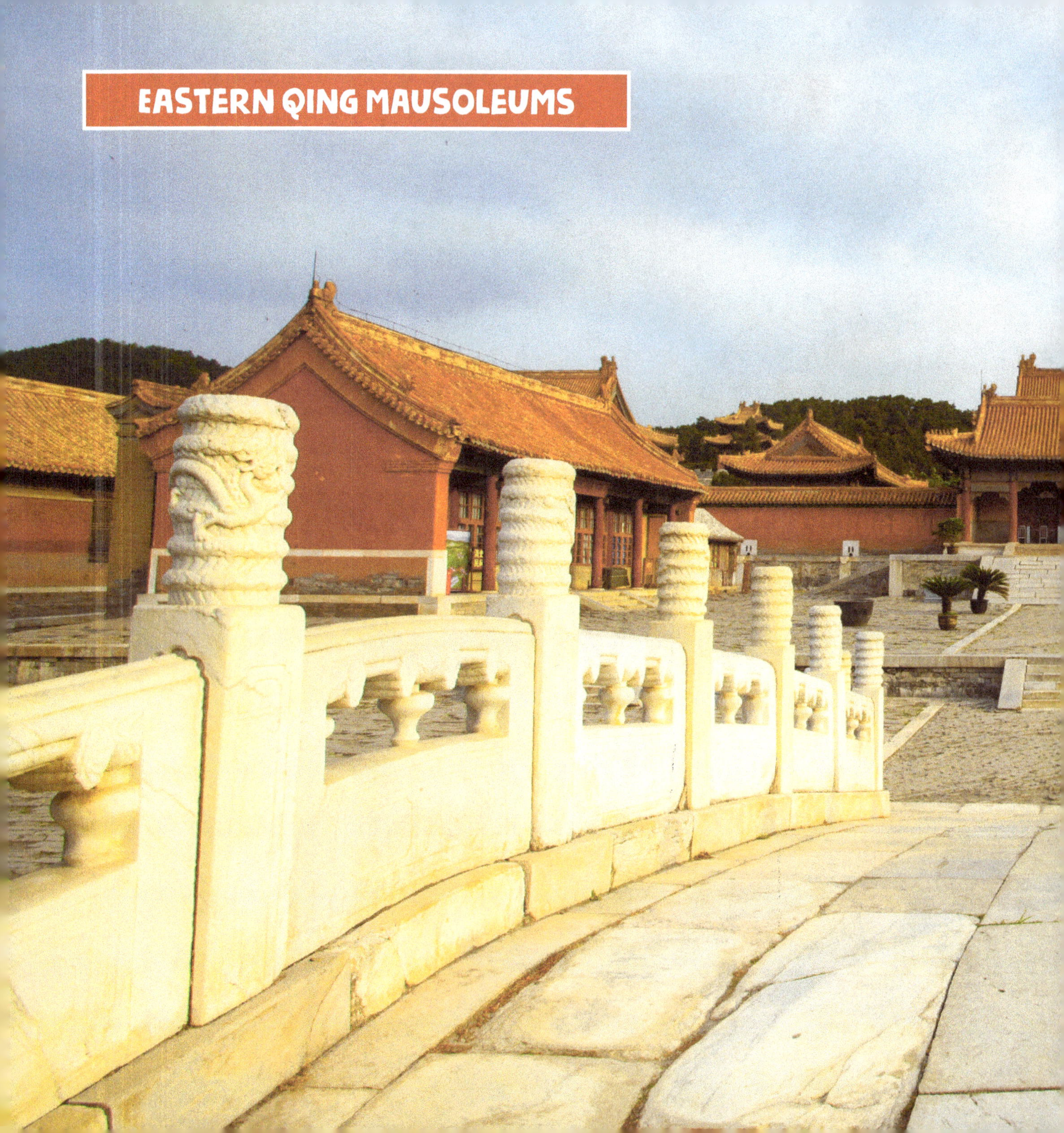

EASTERN QING MAUSOLEUMS

The dynasty and the country were at their greatest strength in the 1750s, but falling revenue from taxes and outside pressure from other countries led China toward a decline. Often Japan and some European countries controlled large parts of China.

In the 20th century there was a move toward a more modern, more democratic form of government. The last emperor resigned in 1912 and China became a republic.

HISTORY AND CULTURE

A nation is much more than its rulers. It is all the people and all their accomplishments, what they do and how they live. Find out more about the great Chinese culture in Baby Professor books like **Who Built the Great Wall of China?, Why do the Chinese Have a Different New Year?, How Did Your Chinese Ancestors Live? and The Chinese Festivals.**

Visit
BABY PROFESSOR
EDUCATION KIDS
www.BabyProfessorBooks.com
to download Free Baby Professor eBooks
and view our catalog of new and exciting
Children's Books

www.ingramcontent.com/pod-product-compliance
Lightning Source LLC
Chambersburg PA
CBHW081713160726
47997CB00024B/2868